mini saga
competition
for Primary Schools from

Tiny Tales

Tyne & Wear

First published in Great Britain in 2007 by
Young Writers, Remus House, Coltsfoot Drive,
Peterborough, PE2 9JX
Tel (01733) 890066 Fax (01733) 313524
All Rights Reserved

Disclaimer
Young Writers has maintained every effort
to publish stories that will not cause offence.
Any stories, events or activities relating to individuals
should be read as fictional pieces and not construed
as real-life character portrayal.

Foreword

Young Writers was established in 1991, with the aim of encouraging the children and young adults of today to think and write creatively. Our latest primary school competition, *Tiny Tales*, posed an exciting challenge for these young authors: to write, in no more than fifty words, a story encompassing a beginning, a middle and an end. We call this the mini saga.

Tiny Tales Tyne & Wear is our latest offering from the wealth of young talent that has mastered this incredibly challenging form. With such an abundance of imagination, humour and ability evident in such a wide variety of stories, these young writers cannot fail to enthral and excite with every tale.

Contents

St Aloysius RC Junior School, Hebburn

St Joseph's RC Primary School, Sunderland

Saltburn Primary School

The Mini Sagas

War Of The Aliens

Suddenly there was a thunderstorm but it was an unusual storm. It struck in the same place twice. 'Robby, Robby.' There was no answer. 'Robby!' still no answer. I searched everywhere then I saw his body. He was dead. What would happen to me …?

Dominic Naylor (9)
Benedict Biscop CE Primary School

The Killer

Sarah knew he was here. She knew she would die and be slaughtered. The man of her nightmares had returned. It was the killer, the executioner of all life forms.

Christopher Simpson (9)
Benedict Biscop CE Primary School

The Hunt

The wolf took one more step towards Ben, his eyes glowing red! The werewolf's drool was making a yellow puddle on the floor.
He awoke suddenly, 'What a wonderful dream!' he sighed. 'It's a full moon tonight, time for the hunt.' He threw his head back, howled and ran.

Sean Nicholson (11)
Benedict Biscop CE Primary School

On Time … After Going Through Hell

Running as fast as he could, he'd lost all hope. Then he came to a halt. Suddenly something emerged from the shadows … What could it be? One breath and he was off. To his surprise the Hell-like figure confronted him! He took a sigh of relief, 'On time!'

Ryan Enguita (11)
Benedict Biscop CE Primary School

New House

Creak, as Samantha opened the old door to her new house. It was late, so she went up into her new room. In the cupboard a strange shadow was emerging from the darkness into the moonlight. What was it? It was getting closer. *'Argh!'* Samantha woke up in bed!

Megan Innes (11)
Benedict Biscop CE Primary School

The Deadly Camp

Andrew stepped out of the rusty train onto the camp, but it didn't look like it. It was a huge authentic castle.
Lifting his hand to knock, he heard a voice.
'Get away!'
Instantly he felt pains in his chest. In excruciating pain he turned, the train was gone!

Elizabeth Quinn (11)
Benedict Biscop CE Primary School

Untitled

As Ben stopped Silver the horse, he saw
something move in the trees next to him. Then
three dogs came and attacked the horse. Ben
tried to stop the dogs. Then they stopped and
went. Ben was relieved.

Christopher Morton (11)
Benedict Biscop CE Primary School

The Beast

Sprinting down the path, Megan felt her heart pounding in her chest. Her legs felt like jelly and, as she glanced behind her, she caught sight of the beast. The roar echoed in Megan's ears as she came face to face with it.
'Finally finished!' Jerry closed his book, smiling.

Samantha Clark (11)
Benedict Biscop CE Primary School

Dalek

It floated with such power. The monster was just staring at me. Why? Suddenly it shouted the most vile word ever. It was 'Exterminate'. It pointed its gun at me. I was scared, then I heard a noise. It shot. I was gone. I was in the clouds, dead.

Connor Buckley (11)
Benedict Biscop CE Primary School

The Battle Of Troy

Hector stood silently underneath the rays of hot sunlight, staring straight into the eyes of the best fighter ever, Achilles. Both men drew their swords. They stood still for a few seconds and then … *crash!* Their swords clashed together. Then suddenly Achilles struck Hector with his sword. It was over.

Jonathan Young (11)
Benedict Biscop CE Primary School

The Duel

Gomad stood face to face with his worst enemy, staring into his deep eyes. He attacked with brute force. As their swords clashed, lightning struck the peak upon which they stood. Gomad stepped back and struck once more, decapitating his opponent … victory was his at last.

Tom Langley (11)
Benedict Biscop CE Primary School

Sunderland Are Going Up

'Bottom left corner,' whispered Joe into Michael's ear. Michael was about to take the penalty to decide if Sunderland were going up. Would he score? Michael ran towards the ball and struck the ball. The ball flew through the air and into the goal. Sunderland were going into the Premiership.

Michael Carr (11)
Benedict Biscop CE Primary School

The Chase

Running like the wind he jumped over the cliff - he grabbed the cliff opposite and pulled himself up. He was still being followed but he could not run anymore. 'Please don't hurt me,' he said. 'I am not going to, the thing is, you dropped your phone.'

Callum Riddell (11)
Benedict Biscop CE Primary School

A New Species

It was awake. It was coming. It was there, a new species of human. 'Oh no, what are you doing? You are destroying the whole lab!' screamed the professor.

Boom! as the wall shattered and the new species of human stomped past the professor and through the shattered wall.

Kieran Ward (10)
Benedict Biscop CE Primary School

The UFO

I was in my tree house then I heard a noise.
I looked out of the window. I saw a UFO. It
landed, aliens came running out and they came
up and up the ladders. I saw their tentacles,
then their eyes and … *'Boo!'* No, it's a monster.

Harry McLaughlan (10)
Benedict Biscop CE Primary School

Afraid!

It was a dark and scary night. There I was, lying there, looking around for ghosts and then suddenly … there was a ghost flying forwards and backwards. It was really scary. I shook my dad and he turned the light on and said, 'It is just the curtains, silly.'

Sophie Shaw (7)
Benedict Biscop CE Primary School

The Lost Locket

Phoebe was wandering in a haunted house, suddenly she let go of her magical locket. Three minutes later, she realised it was gone … she called the detectives. They looked high and low until … *Oooh!* They ran after the sounds. They grabbed the ghost and took the necklace from him.

Lucy Scragg-McCluskey (7)
Benedict Biscop CE Primary School

The Hungry Dinosaurs

Once there was a T-rex, he always ate triceratops, he loved them for his dinner and tea. He crept behind them and ate them; but one day he died from eating too much. Before he died he was the best at catching triceratops. Now everyone had to catch their own triceratops.

Jonathan Fenwick (7)
Benedict Biscop CE Primary School

The Scary Monster

Once there lived a little girl called Red Riding Hood. She was asked to do a job. When she was doing this a monster jumped out. 'Boo!' said the monster. The monster scared Red Riding Hood and she ran away. When she opened her eyes she was at Granny's house.

Jonathan Clark (7)
Benedict Biscop CE Primary School

31

The Scary Birthday Party

When Kitty, Catherine and Dale went to school,
there was nobody there.
Suddenly the floorboards started to creak and
then Kitty, Catherine and Dale started to feel
worried, but then the whole class came out and
said happy birthday to them.

Brooke Coxon (7)
Benedict Biscop CE Primary School

Dark Park

Once there were three girls called Katie, Sarah and Abbie. One day they went camping in the dark park but Fluffy the dog followed. When the girls were asleep something made funny noises outside the tent. The girls thought it was a monster. It was just the dog.

Abbie Little (7)
Benedict Biscop CE Primary School

33

Late

Zzzz! Wake up, it's five minutes to school! Help!
Clothes on, stuff your face, wash it, brush your
teeth. Now let's leg it.
Beep-beep! Oh no, it's gone. Now run round
the corner, down the street, through the gate,
down the corridor. In class! *You're late!*

Hannah Freeman (10)
Benedict Biscop CE Primary School

Mystical Creature

Suddenly I heard a beautiful sound, it sounded mystical and dreamy. I opened my window, it was a gorgeous unicorn with fluttery white wings. I put my hand out to its smooth skin. I climbed on its back and we flew through the stars! It was my mystical creature.

Abigail Chandler (10)
Benedict Biscop CE Primary School

Defeat

I stood there peering at my shattered blade. My arm hurt from the wound my enemy gave me, a sign of defeat. As I looked at my soldiers, dead and wounded, I thought of my destroyed village. There would be no more playful children or anything.

Josh Davies (10)
Benedict Biscop CE Primary School

Dream

'Where am I?' asked Doris curiously.
'You're in Wonderland!' came a voice from
nowhere. 'I was last in my house in Texas but
now I'm here! I want to go home,' cried Doris.
'Doris wake up! Doris!' came a very quiet voice.
'I'm home again!' all of a sudden.

Lauren Sampson (10)
Benedict Biscop CE Primary School

Untitled

I woke up in the middle of the night. I did not know where I was. Then I realised I was at my auntie's house to sleep for the night. I tried to go to sleep but couldn't. I lay with my eyes open, a shadow passed. I was scared.

Ellis Dixon (10)
Benedict Biscop CE Primary School

Boom!

I was so, so tired until, *boom!* I fell to the floor. I was in another world. There were devils and dragons and a shadow coming further and further towards me. I didn't know what it was. Was it a ghost or a devil? Suddenly I heard a loud noise …

Alex Reed (9)
Benedict Biscop CE Primary School

Evana Lives In A Hotel

My name is Evana, I live in Tipton and it's a
very nice place to be. There's Zack and there's
Cody and Maddie and Mosby and London who
love me so well. I am very rich, but sometimes a
witch. My dog is a girl and spins in a whirl.

Gabrielle Middlewood (10)
Benedict Biscop CE Primary School

40

Darkness

My teeth are trembling, my heart is thumping like mad. I can hear something creeping. I am in my room by myself. I am home alone. I open the door, nobody is there. It's pitch-black. I look on the floor, there is a shadow. I look again … a rat!

Megan Buckley (10)
Benedict Biscop CE Primary School

The Haunted Football Ground

It's extremely dark. Midnight approaching, full moon, Hallowe'en ending. I scuttle home quickly. It's the forbidden street. I must go around the long way, past Sunderland football ground. The black cat jumps out at me. I faint. No one knows, my mother will be terrified, I've been gone for hours.

Kaitlin Common (10)
Benedict Biscop CE Primary School

The Tiger

Darkness everywhere, filling the room and painting it black. I couldn't see anything. Suddenly, something emerged from the darkness. I couldn't make it out at first, it was bright orange, white and black. I realised it was a tiger. It started to walk towards me, and started to chase me …

Alexa Clark (10)
Benedict Biscop CE Primary School

43

The Guardian

Once there was a man, the guardian. He slew beasts and monsters with magical swords and muscles. But this beast was different. He was called Fireboo. He was a flicker of fire burning. But then Fireboo started to burn the planet. But then the guardian stabbed him and he froze.

Cameron Chandler (10)
Benedict Biscop CE Primary School

The Forest

There it stood, all alone, in the middle of the forest. I slowly and carefully walked up to it. However, the front door creaked open, I froze! Once the door opened, a rich black shadow stood there. I tried to run but my legs were rooted to the ground.

Kate Robson (10)
Benedict Biscop CE Primary School

The Cold, Dark Forest!

There in the cold, dark forest was silence. You could walk around but not a thing could be seen. Then I saw a little bright light shining upon me. It was too bright for my eyes. Then it disappeared. I wondered what it was. I didn't know, then *crash!*

Lois-Eryn Kirkbride (9)
Benedict Biscop CE Primary School

The Mystery Monster

There it was right in front of me. A bright light. A loud noise. A monster. It got closer and closer and then it dissolved. The door shut. The light switched off. The mystery monster was still there. I looked left and right. It wasn't there. My life was over.

Luke Millward (10)
Benedict Biscop CE Primary School

47

The Quicksand Incident

'Argh!' screamed Tim as he sank deeper into the pit of quicksand. His faint cry for help could only be heard by a young hunter who was also in the forest hunting. *'Argh!'* Tim yelled once again.

The young man ran and ran. Finally he was there, but too late.

James Irwing (11)
Benedict Biscop CE Primary School

Goodbye To Mia, Our Puppy

'Argh! You will be the first puppy to be turned into gold.'
Mia barked to get out of Euphmia's ugly spotted green hands. *A … a … atishoo!* Mia sneezed. She was out of Euphmia's hands. She was somewhere much worse, in the steaming hot cauldron. She knew she was going to die.

Morgan Irvine (10)
Benedict Biscop CE Primary School

49

The Scare In The House

'What is that noise?' shivered James to himself. He was all alone in the house he thought. But he didn't know where the sound was coming from. He was looking everywhere for that noise. Suddenly he heard it again but it was a different noise this time. Then was gone.

Adam Jurgens (10)
Benedict Biscop CE Primary School

The Deadly Forest

I was walking through the forest. I was alone, I was hungry. I found a rabbit, I killed it. I got some wood and made a fire and I cooked it, after I took the skin off. I ate it then I heard a rustle in the bush …

Alex King (10)
Benedict Biscop CE Primary School

The Human Killer

Lisa knew she was here. It was the time, the time when she would die. Every night she would have nightmares and hear funny noises. Windows opened while doors shut. She was definitely here. Shadows on the wall, deep loud footsteps. She was coming. It was the human killer! *Argh!*

Claudia Short (9)
Benedict Biscop CE Primary School

The Lucky Prince

Once upon a time there lived a prince called Jeremy. Jeremy wasn't only handsome he also lived in a huge palace, in a beautiful kingdom. He wanted to marry a princess but there were three princesses. It was confusing. So one day Jeremy took a walk in the woods …

Teagan Brown (8)
Benedict Biscop CE Primary School

Bedtime

It was time for bed at my sleepover party. I turned off the lights and after twenty seconds Hannah screamed. She felt a movement at the end of the blanket, then she felt something touch her feet. I pulled back her blanket and it was my dog!

Kirsten Baillie (9)
Benedict Biscop CE Primary School

Jungalistic Journey

I crept slowly into the amazing jungle. I was astonished to see that there was a forest of trees and a tall canopy stretching high above me; with birds of every colour of the rainbow. There was also a flowing river that sparkled in the sunlight, with twisting vines too!

Madeline Squires (8)
Benedict Biscop CE Primary School

Frankenstein

He roared loudly. Louder than you expected.
Frankenstein roared really loudly. He was
getting closer and closer and closer. He roared
so loudly I nearly hid under my bed.
Finally I walked to him, then I hit him so hard
that he fell to the floor.

James Common (8)
Benedict Biscop CE Primary School

The Ghost

She hid among the gravestones and it happened.
The ghost said, 'I am going to eat you up!' He swept a sword from his coat.
She was not afraid of him. She swept a sword from her dressing gown and cut him in half.
Gone!

Catherine Bradshaw (8)
Benedict Biscop CE Primary School

57

The Sunny Day

The sun shone down on my red-raw shoulders. My ice pop was melting in my hand. I was standing at the end of the funfair with my best friends. Little children were screaming and shouting at the tops of their voices.

Sally Jobling (8)
Benedict Biscop CE Primary School

The Return Of Frankenstein

Creak went the old wooden door. I walked forward into the house, trying not to wake up the evil Frankenstein. I heard a big thud, the floor shook with anger. I wanted to run but I said, 'Hi Mr Frankenstein.'
He said nothing for a second. I ran away.

Sam Quinn (8)
Benedict Biscop CE Primary School

The Dream

The boy raced home, changed, switched on the computer, and looked at his comic. His mum wasn't home. Suddenly the computer sucked him in. The boy found himself making a deal with a pirate. During the game he realised that

…

Suddenly he heard a voice, 'Max! Out of bed!' shouted Mum.

Brian Terry (8)
Benedict Biscop CE Primary School

Monsters Coming

I was there on the landing. There was something coming to get me. It was coming. 'I'm coming!' it roared.
I was scared, so I ran in the bedroom and screamed but then realised it was Mum and Dad trying to scare me. I calmed down and cheered up.

Mathew Jackson (8)
Benedict Biscop CE Primary School

61

The Statue

Bang! The time machine fell in the middle of nowhere. Danny was confused and Doctor Zakle was OK. Danny was in a mood. Then they turned round, a statue sprang out. They jumped out of the time machine and Danny stabbed it. It sprang out at him! Then it disappeared.

Lewis Hodgkinson (8)
Benedict Biscop CE Primary School

Werewolf

One day I was playing in the haunted house
and it all started when I heard a creak upstairs.
It was quiet at first, then got louder and louder
until there was a bang. It was an angry werewolf
storming down the stairs. It came right up to
me, roaring!

Matthew Potts (8)
Benedict Biscop CE Primary School

The Miracle Football Match

It was the Champions League final. Sunderland were in and so was their worst enemy, Newcastle. The match was being played in the biggest stadium in the world, the Aztec Stadium in Mexico. Fifteen minutes had gone and Carloz Edwards scored a goal. Sunderland won the game and the trophy.

Stephen Clark (8)
Benedict Biscop CE Primary School

Tiny Ghosts

There we stood, next to my foster home. It
made me shiver when I looked in. It looked
haunted. It was spooky. When the foster carer
took me to my room, I saw a ghost next to the
fire door. I was cold and so was my sister.
'I'm cold.'

Lauren Patterson (8)
Benedict Biscop CE Primary School

Spooky Tale

As I crept in, I got caught in spiderwebs. Then I saw some Martians and I crept round the corner, but there was the howling of a wolf. I thought for a minute. It was a dog but I ran back to my house and went to my bed.

Calum McCaskill (8)
Benedict Biscop CE Primary School

The Night Trick

It was a dark night. The dog was howling and
then a creak and then blood all over the room.
A shriek and the boy was dead. *'Argh!'*
The boy woke from the nightmare. It was his
sister, she had put ketchup all over the room.
Ha! She laughed.

Bradley Logan (7)
Benedict Biscop CE Primary School

The Story Of The Hungry Blackbirds

One sunny morning in a kitchen as long as a train, a nasty king was waiting for a yummy pie. Suddenly, in a puff of smoke, singing, hopping blackbirds leapt out of the yummy pie. The queen shouted, *'Eeek!'* as the blackbirds pecked off her spotty red nose.

Cassie Pearson (6)
Chopwell Primary School

Poor Humpty Dumpty

One bright morning on a sandy beach,
silly Humpty Dumpty sat on a wobbly wall.
Suddenly, with a loud *crash,* clumsy Humpty
Dumpty tumbled from the steep wall.
Finally a pretty nurse came to rescue him and
took him to hospital and Sellotaped him back
together.

Charlie McGuire Charlton (6)
Chopwell Primary School

The Story Of Humpty Dumpty

One windy morning in a flowery park, silly Humpty Dumpty sat on a wobbly wall. Suddenly with a *bang,* frightened Humpty Dumpty rolled down the steep wall. Luckily Humpty Dumpty was taken to a special hospital, by a magic nurse … who fried and cooked him!

Kate Pugh (5)
Chopwell Primary School

The Story Of Humpty Dumpty

One windy morning in a pretty garden clumsy Humpty Dumpty sat on a gigantic wall. Suddenly, in a gust of wind, Humpty Dumpty tumbled off the gigantic wall. Finally Humpty Dumpty got rushed to hospital by a hungry nurse and she ate him. Yummy!

Joshua Thompson (6)
Chopwell Primary School

The Tale Of Hey Diddle Diddle

One spooky night in the dark, gloomy sky, a jolly cow marched across space. Suddenly the silly cow tried to leap over the moon. *Crash!* The cow fell to an alien planet and broke his funny bone.

Michael Dixon (6)
Chopwell Primary School

Hiss

The hiss grew louder and louder. Max held his
sword harder than ever. The clang of metal
rang around the dark, dingy room. The creak
of wooden doors made him scared. He raised
the sword above his head. The room went quiet
- but he knew it was still there.

Ellen Gibson (10)
Cullercoats Primary School

Indiana Oranges

Indiana Oranges rolled under the closing tomb door. He reached out and grabbed the one and only magic lemon. Suddenly a giant lime came tumbling towards him! He began to run when … *splat!*

That's the downside of being an orange - and for the only magic lemon, he's dead too!

Claire Robinson (10)
Cullercoats Primary School

A Ruby In The Night

Ella slid down the rope silently. She landed, cat-like, on the detailed mosaic floor of the cathedral. The light from the chandelier shone down on the ruby. Ella gazed in awe at the stunning red gem. *No wonder the boss wants it.* She seized the ruby, and was gone.

Phillipa Carson (11)
Cullercoats Primary School

The Beginning Of The End

I gasped as I saw skulls scattered everywhere. I stopped as the Grim Reaper led my way. Fear penetrated through my body. Looking up at the black, starless sky I turned to run back to safety, but I had already been captured by the realm of the afterlife.

Beth Houlis (11)
Cullercoats Primary School

Breathless

A giant snake slithered around the dark cave.
Tom clenched his sword tighter as he watched.
Suddenly the snake caught sight of Tom.
Breathless with fear, Tom yelled as the snake
entwined around his body.
'Tom wake up now!' called Mother.
Phew, how Tom hated bad dreams.

Kieran Bowran (9)
Cullercoats Primary School

Spider Vs Serpent

Silken webs surrounded the battlefield. Swiftly
the giant serpent slithered forward, its steely
eyes surveyed the spider's lair. Suddenly
the king tarantula leapt from the ceiling, its
venomous fangs prepared to bite.
It was a mighty battle, but in the end the snake
tossed the spider aside and declared victory.

Jonathan Cavanagh (11)
Cullercoats Primary School

Silent Death

I am floating and floating, far away, further than you can ever imagine. It's superb, magnificent, unreal. My life isn't worth living anymore, that's why I'm here in this tunnel of everlasting light. I'm going, going … I'm gone.

Victoria Volpe (11)
Cullercoats Primary School

The Magic House

In my street there's a magic house! One day I went in it. The walls were bright but the furniture was black. There was a wish room. I went in it. I sat down and made a wish. The very next day the wish came true!

Anabel Joyce (10)
Cullercoats Primary School

Poor Heart

'I feel frozen,' the poor matchstick girl mumbled to herself. She lit all the matchsticks to keep herself warm. She should have sold them as her father commanded. She had failed. Soon she collapsed and froze to death in the cold night. Her family was puzzled that she died smiling.

Adam Cozens (11)
Hylton Castle Primary School

Cold Heaven

After what seemed to be a very long time of freezing, the poor matchstick girl wept on the streets of London. The girl struggled to sell matches, so she lit them to warm her cold blue fingers. Soon she was frozen again. By night-time she was frozen to death.

Robyn Elvidge (11)
Hylton Castle Primary School

The Matchstick Girl

'My feet are cold as icicles,' a little matchstick girl mumbled as she trudged along an icy path, trying to sell matches. Her dad would beat her if she did not sell any.
She sold none … but instead she collapsed in the cold, dark night and soon froze to death.

Bradley Graham (11)
Hylton Castle Primary School

83

The Girl Who Died With Matches

A young girl, freezing and poor, wandered around the cold damp streets lighting matches, in spite of going home and getting beaten by her dad.
She was lighting matches to keep warm.
She kept on imagining seeing her nana, but suddenly the matchstick girl passed away in the morning.

Liam Nesbitt (11)
Hylton Castle Primary School

Untitled

'My feet are freezing,' the little matchstick girl
cried.
Her parents had filled her pockets with matches
to sell. If she came home with no money her
father would beat her.
She sold no matches, but lit them all in order to
keep warm. She collapsed and froze to death

. . .

Courteney Kincaid (11)
Hylton Castle Primary School

Hide-And-Seek

Tom and Elizabeth had recently moved. Exploring, Tom had an idea. 'Hide-and-seek!' cried Tom. Elizabeth crept up the stairs, cobwebs everywhere. She was terrified. Rushing into the cupboard she slowly closed the door. She tried to push the door, it wouldn't open and she was never found again.

Hannah Richardson (11)
Ryhope Junior School

Argh! There's A Cat In The Kitchen

There's a cat in the kitchen. I know it's stupid, but I'm terrified of them. They're mischievous and sly … *Argh!* It's here, I can see it. It's hissing at me! It would be OK if I were human and scared of cats but, for crying out loud, I'm a dog!

Shelley Dunn (11)
Ryhope Junior School

87

Tokyo Drift

He power slides, narrowly missing the rails.
Next corner, tremendous drift! Oh! A scratch on
the paintwork. Mum'll kill me!
'James, put your cars away!'
'No Mum!'
'Play with them tomorrow!'

Kieran Deacon (11)
Ryhope Junior School

Ice-Cold

Oh no! It's open. The beast has woken!
I look into its shining eye. The beast blows on
me. It's freezing. I don't think I can go on any
longer.
A hand goes in, grabbs the ice cream. The door
shuts. I'm OK now.
Why am I scared of the freezer?

Scott Robson (11)
Ryhope Junior School

The Ascent

Pulling myself up inch by inch. Holding the rope, yelling in pain. Rocks hit my arm. Losing my grip. I had been falling thousands of feet. Singing loudly, 'I'll live forever!'
Suddenly a voice came from below, 'Jonny stop climbing on your bed, and pick up those toys!'

Rebecca Hedley (11)
Ryhope Junior School

The Visitor

Billy sat up. The floorboards creaked. The tap
dripped. It was coming. It was the end.
The bedroom door eerily swung open. Then
darkness. Billy could feel it grapple his throat.
Then it punched him in the eye.
'Oh pack it in, Sis, can't I get some sleep,
please!'

Jordan Bray (11)
Ryhope Junior School

Terror

I tried not to think about it as I got into the car. I thought it was going to be OK, but when we parked in the car park I saw a gang of people. The biggest one stared at me and I knew it was going to be bad.

Matthew Young (11)
Ryhope Junior School

Untitled

One night I was sailing near the Bermuda Triangle, I saw a ship floating. The words read Marie Celeste. The lifeboat was gone. The ship was moving. There was nobody steering it. On the deck restaurant there was no one eating but the meals were on the table to eat.

Charlotte Thompson (10)
Ryhope Junior School

What On Earth!

Mrs Webster left her class for five minutes while she took the register down to the office. But when she returned not one child from her class was there. She searched everywhere - (well that's what she said). She was actually happy to lose her class. The little devils.

Dayna Barkel (11)
Ryhope Junior School

94

A Whale Of A Time

At that moment I dived into the sea. The cold water felt good. I went under and saw it. A blue whale. How great it felt to see one in real life. Then it happened, I was going down and couldn't breath. It was a shark! Then I woke up.

Adam Robson (11)
Ryhope Junior School

95

Scared Of Heights

My heart pounded. Sweat dripped from my head. My knees felt like jelly. Each step was even more frightening. My fingers gripping onto the handrail. The steps seemed to get steeper and steeper. I couldn't go any further; then I realised I was at the bottom of the lighthouse.

Laura Mitchell-Hall (11)
Ryhope Junior School

The Flight

We took off into the sky. My ears popped. We were let out of our seats after a short time in the air. The captain turned the seat belt sign back on. I could feel the plane dropping. Everyone was worried for their lives. *Bang!* The engine blew out …

Connor Sanderson (11)
Ryhope Junior School

97

The Flying Saucer

There it was, the flying saucer! It landed in a field. It was so loud I blocked my ears and the glow of the engine died. The door opened and there was a big black shadow. It looked at me and walked towards me. I was shaking.

Daniel Casey (11)
Ryhope Junior School

The Spell

A puff of smoke wandered up from the cauldron into my eyes. The cat's paw was the main ingredient and it worked like a charm. It was tasty and the spell of a lifetime, just like it said in the book 'Family Recipes'.

Jadene Elliott (10)
Ryhope Junior School

The Aliens

There were green lights in the sky, no one knew
if it was a plane or not. No one knew if it was
a UFO then it happened - aliens walked to the
humans and greeted them.

Thomas Keen (11)
Ryhope Junior School

Bermuda Triangle

On the aeroplane I was sweating nervously.
I jumped on my mum and dad's knees,
surrounded by my sister and my brother,
every single one of us screaming. The pilot
had just said we were travelling over the
Bermuda Triangle. I had heard stories of people
disappearing …

Channon Moore (11)
Ryhope Junior School

101

Bang Goes The Wizard

Into the pot they go. One after another; frogs' legs, tail of a newt, tail of a dog, liver of a dragon, tiger's stripes, a star from space, a wizard's wand, a fish's tail and a turtle's head. *Bang!*
A bit more turtle's head. *Bang!* OK, no turtle's head. *Bang!*

Josh Peacock (11)
Ryhope Junior School

The Jumping Leprechaun

One day Jack was jumping through the wood with a smile on his face and some gold in his pocket. He was the happiest leprechaun in the whole wide world of leprechauns. I became his best friend because he was lonely and I felt very pitiful. We played together.

Leah Errington (10)
Ryhope Junior School

The Comet

The vast creature rose from the forest, pushing aside the trees in its path like a child throwing a tantrum. As he looked up he saw the fireball coming straight for his territory. The creature panicked. The beast would die. He then tripped over a small rock and died.

Joe Helyer (11)
Ryhope Junior School

I'm Terrified

I'm really afraid of water. I lost my fear on holiday though. I was on the poolside when a football from, guess who, my dad, flew towards me, making me duck. When a bee stung me! I fell and swam! I got over my fear. I'm terrified of bees now.

Nathan Lough (11)
Ryhope Junior School

Rich Jack!

I'm rich but I was poor. Let me tell you my story. I sold my cow for magic beans. I showed my mother and she chucked them out of the window. Those beans made a stalk. I climbed up and fought with a giant. Climbed down. I was a winner.

Craig Taylor (10)
Ryhope Junior School

Cinderella Poem

I walked out from the cellar singing a song,
I saw a carriage driving along bearing my
one true love, the prince. His beauty made
me wince, for today we declared the love
we shared. Because of one glass shoe, I'm
standing here in a wedding dress that is blue.

Adrienne Littler (10)
Ryhope Junior School

Hickory Dickory Dock

Once there was a little mouse living under the floorboards. Every day at five to one, the little mouse would come out, go to the passage then to the grandfather clock. He would climb up it. Then when it struck one he would run back down into the floorboards.

May Godfrey (10)
Ryhope Junior School

Dragon Slayer

One miserable day a man went to slay a dragon. He packed up lots of food and armour and so he sailed to an island called Crandor. It was like a giant volcano and had huge monsters. He climbed to the top of the volcano, went inside and slew the dragon.

Connor Lamb (9)
Ryhope Junior School

Jack And Jill

In the morning Jack and Jill ran up the hill to the well. Jack never knew his shoe was untied. He tumbled down the hill. Jill ran down with a bucket of water then took Jack home. The next day a doctor came and he said, 'Jack broke his head!'

Amy Rowe (10)
Ryhope Junior School

My Secret Unicorn Helps A Friend

Lauren gets a pony and finds it's a unicorn. Her friend Mel's pony won't jump. Lauren goes with Twilight to teach them how to jump.
There's a stormy night and lightning strikes. It sets fire to the shed where the ponies are stuck. They jump over the fire. *Hooray!*

Natasha Barkel (9)
Ryhope Junior School

Aeroplanes

It tossed, it turned, I didn't like it. I stood, I fell. It felt like I was trapped. It was impossible to tell how high I was now. My mum just said to keep myself occupied, but I couldn't. Why am I so scared of aeroplanes? *Help! Get me off!*

Bethany Hartley (11)
Ryhope Junior School

The Death Ride

Argh! I nervously gripped onto the safety bar of the Death Ride roller coaster. Round and upside down it twisted and twirled. My heartbeat got faster. Sweat dripped off my forehead. I screamed hysterically until my voice was lost. Finally, it ended. I shouted unexpectedly, 'Cool, let's do it again!'

Hannah Barkel (11)
Ryhope Junior School

The Forest

I am terrified in the forest all by myself. 'What's that rustling in the trees?' I say to myself. 'Is that whiskers tickling my leg?' I turn round quickly, I see a rabbit. Now I don't feel so scared, with one of my favourite animals. I will take it home.

Amy Hibbert (11)
Ryhope Junior School

Little Red Riding Hood

A girl was on her way to Granny, with some biscuits covered in a blanket; she was walking along. She eventually reached Granny's. She went in: sharp teeth, bad breath, screwed-up eyes! My grandma? Suddenly jumping out. The woodcutter. *Hooray!*

Courtney Robinson (10)
Ryhope Junior School

The Mystery Creature

I turned the corner. There she was. I felt a shiver down my spine. I looked at her, then ran as fast as I could. I turned into my street, thinking I'd lost her. There was a loud cry. I looked up and there she was … Kate, the school bully.

Lauren Haggerton (9)
Ryhope Junior School

The Bermuda Triangle

It was a clear day. Not a cloud in the sky. The plane jetted over the dazzling ocean. Suddenly the dials spun out of control and the plane began to plummet. Back at the control tower the plane had disappeared from the radar. Yet another casualty of the Bermuda Triangle.

Ross Patterson (8)
Ryhope Junior School

117

The Mystery Creature

There was a loud scream. I froze with fear.
There was sweat dripping from my head. I felt
someone swoop past. I stepped forward. Then I
heard another scream. I reached out. Someone
was there. I ran into a tall building. I was frozen
in a slimy mass of glue.

Megan Keen (9)
Ryhope Junior School

The Creepy Hand

He pointed his finger at the girl. She quickly turned away but it was too late. She had turned into a small green frog, or had she? It was true she was no longer there, but wasn't that Jimmy Banks removing the lid from the tank containing the frogs.

Anna Small (9)
Ryhope Junior School

Magic Spell

The slime slithered up the wall. The spell had gone terribly wrong. A huge ugly monster dived out of the slime. I waved my magic wand. The monster turned uglier, meaner and bigger. It walked towards me with giant claws and grinned. It had an evil look on its face.

Bradley Slee (9)
Ryhope Junior School

The Experiment That Went Wrong

Doctor Benny decided to perform an experiment. He mixed two potions together. They fizzed and sizzled. There was a loud bang! Doctor Benny scrambled out of the room. His hair was black and sticking up. A lot of science things were unable to be used. The laboratory was beyond recognition.

Marc Smith (9)
Ryhope Junior School

121

A Sporting Disaster

It was time for football practice. I put my kit on and hurried to the field. We chose our teams. The game started. Someone passed the ball. I ran towards it. The next thing I knew I was waking up with a splitting headache. I'd run into a goalpost.

Nathan Ferguson (9)
Ryhope Junior School

A Weird Worry

Hooray! The beast had gone.
We were playing. My friend needed a torch to
finish the game. She went to get one.
Three hours had passed and still no sight of
her! Could it be that there was a real monster
out there? I started to shiver. I felt alone!

Louisa Surtees (9)
Ryhope Junior School

Was It A Dream?

One dark night I heard a sound. It was coming
from the attic. I went to investigate.
I opened the door, pulled down the ladder and
climbed up. I saw my cute cuddly toys having a
party. They were singing, 'YMCA'.
After the party I went straight back to bed.

Calum Harrison (8)
Ryhope Junior School

When Bubbles Found Arnie

One day there were two cats called Arnie and Bubbles. Arnie went out, so Bubbles went to find him. Bubbles started to look for him next door. The grass was so long it tickled her nose. She sneezed!

'Bless you!' said a voice. It was Arnie, also in the grass.

Amy Green (8)
Ryhope Junior School

A Day In The Park

One day Lucy and Abby went to the park. First they went on the swings, then the slide, because they both liked slides the best. They were having so much fun. Then it started to rain, so they ran all the way home. They were just in time for tea.

Ellie Brazier (7)
Ryhope Junior School

Untitled

The sweat dripped down my neck as I waited for the train. It finally got here. The train started and we went through the tunnel. There was a bang! The train was too tall. It crashed into a wall. Now I'm the only one left.

Danielle Anderson (11)
Ryhope Junior School

Volcano Erupts

I'm pouring with sweat, nobody knows what will happen to us. The volcano is erupting, all I can see is people running for their lives. We are trying to get to the furthest place away from here, but I can't run fast enough. I can see it, *argh!* It's here.

Elizabeth Richardson (9)
St Aloysius RC Junior School, Hebburn

A Dream Come True

The beach was beautiful, the sand so gold,
the sea so blue, it's like a dream come true.
The sun was setting in the dazzling sky. I lay
and watched the night arrive. I fell asleep lying
against the sand. Waking up to find … it had all
been a dream.

Rachel Fletcher (8)
St Aloysius RC Junior School, Hebburn

The Aliens Have Landed

Once there lived a man called Paul. He was a scientist!
One day he saw a flashing light flying by so he decided to follow it! When he got closer, he realised that it was an alien ship so he was going to examine it, when suddenly something jumped out!

Owen Carroll (8)
St Aloysius RC Junior School, Hebburn

The Shadow
In The Dark

The street was dark, there was a bit of light from a broken street lamp. I started to feel scared, I walked faster. I was by myself, I didn't look back as I thought I could hear something but, as I slowed down, I noticed it was my shadow.

Daniel Wilkinson (8)
St Aloysius RC Junior School, Hebburn

Centre Of Attention

Once again he knew as soon as they spotted him they would laugh. Everyone would point and laugh at his face, at his clothes and his shoes. He took a deep breath ready to face them all and then smiled uncontrollably. Jojo the clown loved being part of the circus.

Jack Kiely (9)
St Aloysius RC Junior School, Hebburn

A Bad Experiment!

My lips trembled, I shivered inside, I started to sweat, fidgeted all over. I was breathing so heavily, couldn't sit still. Then it happened, it all went wrong. I knew it was a bad experiment. The plane took off, I was screaming inside. I knew this was a bad idea!

Catherine Riley (9)
St Aloysius RC Junior School, Hebburn

My Big Sister

My big sister is horrid, I asked for a pencil.
'Go away,' she shouted, I did.
I really needed to stand up to her so later I
asked again, you want to know what happened
don't you? Well you can't, it was too much of an
accident to tell.

Rosie McCaffery (9)
St Aloysius RC Junior School, Hebburn

The Sweet Shop

Paige went into a sweet shop which looked tiny and dull from the outside but the inside was huge and colourful. Everything was made out of sweets and chocolate, even the counter was made out of candyfloss. Paige was the first person to walk through the sweet shop doors.

Jodie English (10)
St Aloysius RC Junior School, Hebburn

The Mysterious Alien Force

Flying across the universe, searching for the perfect planet for its mission. Most worlds have felt its terrible power. It soared past Saturn, its rings shattered, even the largest meteor crumbled when it forced its way through, its trail of destruction was sequenced and the next target was Planet Earth.

John Lewis (10)
St Aloysius RC Junior School, Hebburn

The Big Win

On Friday the cross-country team were ready to go to the riverside. The race was about to start, ready, steady, go and they were gone. Dylan 3rd, Liam 2nd, it was the last leg, everyone was waiting for him. He was 1st, they had won, they cheered.

Liam O'Brien (10)
St Aloysius RC Junior School, Hebburn

The Haunted House

One day Ablominus and Emmanlander were playing when Ablominus decided to explore the house just streets away. Emmanlander followed Ablominus so when they reached the house they searched top to bottom, then *argh!* It was Emmanlander. Ablominus came to the room, then … 'No!' then nobody saw them ever again.

Jack Horne (10)
St Aloysius RC Junior School, Hebburn

Concert Crisis!

The whole of the arena fell quiet. You could not hear a sound. Why? The lead singer had lost her voice; what a disaster!
The problem was solved. They got some of the children from the audience to sing. I was picked and it was the best concert ever!

Anna Godfrey (9)
St Aloysius RC Junior School, Hebburn

The Weird Dream

Jodie always had funny dreams but this was the funniest when she was in the swimming baths and she found a tap on the swimming pool. Next she noticed that there was hardly any space to swim. Suddenly she woke up and found that she had been in the bath.

Paige Stafstrom (9)
St Aloysius RC Junior School, Hebburn

The Haunted House

As I entered the spooky, dark mansion, the door creaked and the handle fell off and hit against the floor. I heard a noise, I was so scared, I tried to run back out but the door was suddenly locked. I turned around and saw something. *Argh!*

Daniel Bryden (10)
St Aloysius RC Junior School, Hebburn

The Ghost Train

Two workmen were inspecting the tracks when they heard a train. They looked up, there was nothing there, suddenly they heard a whistle and it was getting closer and closer, a big gust of wind rushed past them, the signals turned green, the workmen were never to be seen again.

Luke Phillipson (10)
St Aloysius RC Junior School, Hebburn

The Haunted House

I stood in front of the door shaking, I couldn't get to sleep, a tale about a little boy that was killed spooked me. I got up and heard strange noises. I packed my case and ran! *Argh!* A white ghostly head stared at me, I ran away, scared stiff.

Jade Spencer (10)
St Aloysius RC Junior School, Hebburn

The Sp-Sp-Spooky Train

I received a letter saying that I won a competition and that I had to travel to London, making my own way … by *train!* I walked to the train station, I shivered, the hairs on my neck stood up, I heard voices … I was the only one on the train!

Megan Evans (10)
St Aloysius RC Junior School, Hebburn

The Spooky Castle

There was a spooky castle at Horror Drive, I went inside to have a look, there was a blood-curdling noise, I saw what could have been a ghost. The ghost was white, I was scared, I shivered, I ran out and never went there again.

Joseph Whitfield (10)
St Aloysius RC Junior School, Hebburn

The Spooky Castle

I opened the door to Spooky Castle, I could hear screaming spirits. *Drip, drop*, it was only the tap but I was terrified. The door slammed behind me … and then my mum shouted upstairs, 'Shanice, it's time for school.' It was just a dream. That was the worst ever!

Shanice Baird (10)
St Aloysius RC Junior School, Hebburn

A Scary Journey

I received a letter to confirm my journey on a train to Southam.
When I arrived I heard noises like ghosts and voices going *oooohhh!* Things were worse, I was alone. My heart was beating like a drum, I felt like screaming for help. I was locked inside.
Somebody help!

Josh O'Connor (10)
St Aloysius RC Junior School, Hebburn

Haunted House

As I entered the haunted house, shivers ran up my spine, I tiptoed quietly across the squeaky floorboards and a colony of bats flew over my head. Phew, that was a close one. Suddenly out of nowhere, jumped something strange. 'Argh!' I ran out of the house never to return.

Rhiannon Noble (10)
St Aloysius RC Junior School, Hebburn

148

Michael's Rescue

It was Sport's Day, Michael was entered in the hurdles, Michael began his 400 metre hurdles very well but it went wrong when he tripped up. Michael needed help and help came, it was from Superboy. Superboy picked him up and flew Michael to the finish.
Michael had won.

Kyle Donaghy (10)
St Aloysius RC Junior School, Hebburn

The Black Dogs Of Bungay

Hounds appear in a dramatic flash and disappear into mist. The ghostly hounds are connected to memories of wicked humans. Bungay is popular for black dogs. A nasty man called Hugh joined forces with a rebel, Geffrey de Mandeville. Thirty years later, Hugh died and haunted places as a hound!

Jessie Horne (11)
St Aloysius RC Junior School, Hebburn

The Giant Jack O'Legs

Jack O'Legs was a thieving giant man, when he noticed the people in Weston had no flour he stole some from the bakers, his punishment was death. He wanted to be buried where his arrow landed, which was Weston Church Tower, so that was the story of giant Jack O'Legs.

Bryony Lee (11)
St Aloysius RC Junior School, Hebburn

151

Tom Hickathrift And The Ogre Of The Smeeth

Tom was a strong giant, people were amazed by his strength. A brewer paid Tom to take his beer to Wisbech, telling him to avoid the ogre in the marshland. Tom ignored this and saw the ogre. Tom killed the ogre, went in its cave, found treasures, then became rich.

Emily Cochrane (11)
St Aloysius RC Junior School, Hebburn

Pandora's Box

Zeus hated Prometheus. Zeus created Pandora. Beautiful but deceitful, Pandora was sent to Prometheus' brother who immediately fell in love and married her. For their wedding present, Zeus sent a box and forbid them to open it. One day Pandora couldn't help herself, she opened it, releasing the evil spirits.

Eve Robinson (11)
St Aloysius RC Junior School, Hebburn

A Witch In A Bottle

A weird woman named Sally was burnt to death, accused of witchcraft. Therefore, she made a threat of revenge on the monks who killed her. Mysterious things began to happen. A palmer was called out and he put witches' lure (poison) in a bottle, he had defeated the wicked witch.

Alexandra Nesbitt (11)
St Aloysius RC Junior School, Hebburn

Theseus And The Minotaur

Theseus was an extremely strong man who wanted to stop people from Athens being sent to Crete to be killed by the Minotaur, so Theseus decided to go so he could defeat the Minotaur.
In the end, Theseus eventually managed to destroy the Minotaur by giving it a memorable hit.

Liam MacLennan (11)
St Aloysius RC Junior School, Hebburn

The Story Of Martin Molloy

I'm reading a book about an old man who hunted and killed little children. He had black hair, always wore dark-coloured clothes and carried a dagger. He was called Martin Molloy. *Creak!* The door is opening. *Argh!* Next morning all that's found in my room are blood-splattered pages.

Thomas Richardson (9)
St Aloysius RC Junior School, Hebburn

Little Bow-Bet

Little Bow-Bet has lost her pets and doesn't know where to find them, so she runs home and sits at the door and they come running behind her.

Ailsa Samuels (9)
St Aloysius RC Junior School, Hebburn

Dream Team!

The football stuck to my feet like glue, I ran like
the wind down the pitch while the crowd roared.
I dribbled the ball past Ronaldo and Rooney.
I took aim, and the ball was in the back of the
net. *Goal!*
I suddenly woke up, what a fantastic dream!

Dominic Chapman (9)
St Aloysius RC Junior School, Hebburn

My Pet Pup

I always dreamt of having a pet puppy and today my mum is buying me one! I've decided to call him Fluff because he is fluffy. He is a Border collie. I love him!
I look after Fluff, (apart from when I'm at school, then Gran cares for him)!

Hannah Henley (9)
St Aloysius RC Junior School, Hebburn

My Football Dream

I walked onto the football pitch so proud as captain. The game started, soon we were two goals ahead. Then I fell and injured my ankle. I was taken to hospital and put to sleep to have it tended to, I woke up in my own bedroom. What a dream!

Nathaniel Docherty (9)
St Aloysius RC Junior School, Hebburn

My Rabbit

My rabbit, Poppy, was sitting on the step. Off she jumped into the mud and got all mucky and brown. She rolled around in the mud and got all sticky and smelly. She came out and jumped about. She flicked the mud all over me and I began to shout.

Abbie Jackson (8)
St Aloysius RC Junior School, Hebburn

The Naughty Rabbit

One sunny day there was a bouncy brown rabbit in the sun, this rabbit loved broccoli and carrots. The rabbit was very naughty and cheeky so it stole a Sunday dinner just to eat carrots and broccoli. The rabbit did wrong and its owner forgave him. Then everyone lived happily.

Emily Cawkwell (9)
St Aloysius RC Junior School, Hebburn

My Magic Spell

My spell needs frog eyes, dead spiders and donkey heads but I need some gunpowder from the back of a farm. Now I'm here, I grab a handful but suddenly someone sets a match on the gunpowder … *Kaboom!* I'm dead.

Andrew Firth (10)
St Aloysius RC Junior School, Hebburn

163

Little Red Riding Hood

Once there was a girl called Red Riding Hood, who visited her grandma, she was in the wood when a wolf saw her, she arrived at her grandma's but she looked different. As she walked closer, the wolf jumped out and ate her, people heard screaming and killed the wolf.

Ellie Smith (9)
St Aloysius RC Junior School, Hebburn

Three Little Pigs

One day there was three pigs and they were building a house. One made theirs out of sticks, the other made theirs out of bricks and straw. The day the wolf came and tried to blow it down, he tried the next house, so he went home.

Charnelle Carter (10)
St Aloysius RC Junior School, Hebburn

Little Red

I am going to Granny's house, a wolf jumped out, he asked me 'Where are you going?' I told him I walked in the bedroom, she wasn't well. She was a mess, it was the wolf. 'Help!' I shouted, someone came in, he killed the wolf with a sword.

Liam Heywood (10)
St Aloysius RC Junior School, Hebburn

A Bizarre Experiment

I was walking to school and I saw a rabbit and I was allergic to rabbits, then I ran but the rabbit ran too so I stopped and then ran but then I realised if I run, the rabbit runs, if I stop, the rabbit stops, I was at school.

Jack Davison (10)
St Aloysius RC Junior School, Hebburn

Little Red Riding Hood

One day Red went down to the woods to get to her grandma's. She walked and saw a wolf so she quickly ran, when she got there, Grandma looked different, she went up to her, she looked - it was that wolf! She screamed, the woodcutter came and killed the wolf.

Kelsa George (10)
St Aloysius RC Junior School, Hebburn

The Bizarre Experiment

It was the first time I walked to school. It was a world with strangers and trees. A small creature jumped out of the gate, it was a black, hairy and small experiment but when I asked, they said it was a spider.
I believe it was a bizarre experiment.

Joseph Lamb (10)
St Aloysius RC Junior School, Hebburn

Three Goats

There once lived three goats, one day they decided to cross the river to eat the fresh grass, but there was a troll. The troll let the first two goats cross but the troll made Big Goat furious and he head-butted the troll over the side of the bridge.

Rachel Turnbull (10)
St Aloysius RC Junior School, Hebburn

The Race's Mystery

The race was three days ago. The winner wasn't to be seen, he was miles ahead of anyone else. He even broke a new record for a mile. However, he never showed up for his prize. He ran straight off; the prize was £1 million. Policemen were looking for him.

Lauren Kyle (10)
St Aloysius RC Junior School, Hebburn

The Haunted Palace

It's Christmas Eve, there was a little girl and boy, they were outside. They found a gate, it was open, so they went in. Inside they climbed the staircase and found a room. In it was one thing, an expensive vase, the girl broke it and ran away.

Laura Phipps (10)
St Aloysius RC Junior School, Hebburn

A Ride With The Devil

Colonel lived at the old hill, Ranworth. He would bully. In December a meeting was held, he challenged his neighbour to race, he pulled out his pistol and shot the horse. New Year's Eve was the night of the banquet, the door suddenly flung open, Colonel faded into the darkness.

Kieran Lawson (11)
St Aloysius RC Junior School, Hebburn

173

Little Red Riding Hood

Little Red Riding Hood was taking a basket to her grandma but got followed by a wolf. The wolf disguised himself as her grandma to trick and to eat Little Red Riding Hood, but a woodchopper was nearby and he came in, killed the wolf and then freed grandma.

Chloe Dunn (11)
St Aloysius RC Junior School, Hebburn

The Vampire In The Haunted Mansion

One day Grace and Jo went to their uncle's mansion but he was out so they waited in his house. They went up to the haunted room and something moved, then their uncle John and Emily came in and they all ran upstairs but Uncle John never came back.

Emily Robson (10)
St Joseph's RC Primary School, Sunderland

175

Untitled

One fine day there was a little boy named Tom, he was having a dream, he dreamt that he was on a football pitch, Cristiano Ronaldo came over, 'Hello little boy!' he said, 'let's go beat Lampard and Robben, OK?'
'John get out of bed, now!' shouted his mother.

Ryan Green (10)
St Joseph's RC Primary School, Sunderland

The Stranger From Space

Whoosh! Crash! went the rocket. It landed in the middle of a back street. The rocket door burst open and smoke came rushing out, then a dark figure came to the door, it was big and green with an oval face, it stepped out and entered Planet Earth. *Yikes!*

Evadne Nelson (10)
St Joseph's RC Primary School, Sunderland

Untitled

I had a dream I was in an enchanted forest. Me, Emily and Erin were wandering around when we saw a glow in the trees. We walked over and we saw a full group of fairies flying and fluttering their wings. We were amazed, there was over 100!

Grace Robson (10)
St Joseph's RC Primary School, Sunderland

The Disaster

The car was going faster than it was supposed
to. The engine had conked out. The Porsche
was skidding far.
The police came to check. The man was
seriously injured. An ambulance came to
help. They took him to hospital. He needed
treatment, when he got there, he was safe.

Alex Bayliss (10)
St Joseph's RC Primary School, Sunderland

Emily, The Lucky Princess

A couple of years ago, Emily's father passed away and she was stuck with her horrible stepmother. One day, Emily was in love, it was love at first sight. Soon they married and moved away and, in the end, Emily had three kids and Emily lived happily ever after.

Jo Nelson (10)
St Joseph's RC Primary School, Sunderland

Princess Melody

Queen of the castle with pixies to help, going to Florida twice a month, what else do I need? But then a large green dragon came, lifted me off my feet, my palms sweating, then my mum shouted, 'Erin, hurry up you will be late for school!' I just smiled.

Erin Christina Cliff (10)
St Joseph's RC Primary School, Sunderland

Overboard Nightmare

I was shaking, sliding everywhere, the waves were splashing me. I was drenched! Things were falling all over me, I was petrified, I was screaming, then someone pushed me over and banged my head. I fell overboard.
'Wake up Sam!'
I wish I didn't toss and turn so much.

Lauren Bramley (10)
St Joseph's RC Primary School, Sunderland

182

Dino's Paradise

It was the age of the dinosaurs. For the
dinosaurs T-Rex was king.
There were three different groups: herbivore,
omnivore and carnivore.
Suddenly a fight broke out, the king and a
triceratops, not long into it and already the
triceratops was dead! The king rapidly feasted
on the dead carcass.

Alex Moore (10)
St Joseph's RC Primary School, Sunderland

My Worst Fear

I was standing on the stage, my hands shaking as I saw the audience staring at me, they were all waiting for me to say something. I tried to say my lines but nothing came out of my mouth. Just then, I woke up to find it was a dream.

Rebecca Burnett (10)
St Joseph's RC Primary School, Sunderland

The Wrong Spell

Once there lived a magician that couldn't stop showing off. One day he decided to join the circus. Everyone was so jealous that he could do magic and started to pick on him. The magician was so cross that when he did a spell it all went wrong. Suddenly - *Bang!*

Holly Riddell (10)
St Joseph's RC Primary School, Sunderland

The Haunted Dream

On the night that Steven fell asleep, he had the most haunting and weirdest dream ever and here it is, it was midnight, he could hear the leaves crackle, also trees shake, suddenly he could see a grave with his name on it, then Steven woke up.

Joseph Bowens (10)
St Joseph's RC Primary School, Sunderland

The Broken Staircase

As I stepped on the first step, the whole staircase creaked and wobbled, I took another step and another, I trembled with fear. Suddenly the staircase collapsed and I went tumbling down, down, until I hit the floor with a thud. *I think we need a new staircase* I thought.

Eve Watson (9)
St Joseph's RC Primary School, Sunderland

The Lift

The floor was rumbling down, down. Down I went. I was pressing the *up* button but I was still going down. I heard a *tick-tock, tick-tock* but there was no clock. I looked around but there was nothing there. Then I heard the doors opening and there stood Mum.

Liam Scullion (9)
St Joseph's RC Primary School, Sunderland

A Journey To Space

Once upon a time there was a boy who went to space in a rocket with his dog Terry. He went to the most dangerous planet, it was Planet Jez. He was stuck on Planet Jez, in a hole, however an alien came and saved him and he went back.

Arun Thomas (8)
St Joseph's RC Primary School, Sunderland

A Fright In The Night

I saw it, the biggest shadow ever! I ran in shock. I hid under my blanket, but it was there. It barked at me and then I realised it was my puppy Shaggy. I put him to bed, night-night Shaggy.

Sam Blakey (8)
St Joseph's RC Primary School, Sunderland

The Gloomy Night
In The Loft

In the gloomy night I was afraid, it was damp, I felt scared and alone. My spine was tingling. I was afraid. I laid my head on the loft floor. *Argh!* My mam opened the door and gave me warm milk and cookies. I was astonished.

Aidan Baldasera (8)
St Joseph's RC Primary School, Sunderland

191

The Old Bears

In a cottage lived two old bears, it was their birthday the next day, their family were planning a meal for them. They went to a restaurant for tea, they had spaghetti Bolognese, they had the best birthday ever.

Anna Foster (9)
St Joseph's RC Primary School, Sunderland

The Haunted House

One day when I was walking home, I saw a creepy old house so I went in and I saw a ghost, then I went up the stairs and shivered with fear. In front of me was a werewolf so I ran away.

Connor Vipond (8)
St Joseph's RC Primary School, Sunderland

Alone In The Dark

In the dark woods I ambled along the path in fear, hearing the owl and bat, having strange and scary feelings. I stamped on the fallen leaves and heard them crunching. Then I looked behind, it was a lost dog!

Jaisil Joseph (8)
St Joseph's RC Primary School, Sunderland

Christmas Day

I woke up on Christmas Day and saw the magic Christmas key. The carrot was eaten, so was the mince pie and the sherry was gone. I went into the front room and there were all my presents, *wow!* I opened my smallest present first, it was a DS, 'Thanks!'

Emma Ford (9)
St Joseph's RC Primary School, Sunderland

195

The Bermuda Triangle

The plane lights dimmed, the controls went haywire, everybody began to scream. Sweat dripped off my face. I began to shiver because we were flying into the Bermuda Triangle! The plane began to drop down into the deep sea. The plane got out of the triangle, we were safe.

Claudia Spoor (8)
St Joseph's RC Primary School, Sunderland

A Spell That Goes Wrong

One sunny day, a witch was making a spell for a young girl to turn her into a scary mermaid. When the witch found the girl, she cast the spell on her. The witch said, 'Ah Keyey Penjen al,' but the girl didn't turn into a scary mermaid.

Emma Davies (9)
St Joseph's RC Primary School, Sunderland

Untitled

One day I was in the garden and I felt something on my leg. When I looked down I saw a big hairy spider and I was really scared! I ran into my house and then I saw it on my table, I screamed loud and then I killed it.

Laura Hedley (8)
St Joseph's RC Primary School, Sunderland

The Big Black Spider

One day there was a big black scary spider in my bathroom, the whole family was too scared to go to the toilet or shower or even the bath, everybody hated us because we never had a bath, until I barged into the bathroom and killed the spider.

David Vincent (9)
St Joseph's RC Primary School, Sunderland

Sellios And The Minotaur

Stellios and the mighty warrior walked though the mysterious cave, he was making a note of where he had been by dropping string where he walked. Suddenly a giant monster leapt out at him, *this must be the Minotaur,* Stellios thought. He jumped at the Minotaur and ran at it.

Michael Wilkinson (11)
St Joseph's RC Primary School, Sunderland

Humpty Dumpty

Humpty Dumpty climbed the wall and sat there for a day, then he got bored and pushed himself off and is scrambled eggs today.

Matthew Sweeney (11)
St Joseph's RC Primary School, Sunderland

Christmas

Wrapping paper flew everywhere. It was Christmas morning, necklaces, bracelets, sweets but Lola knew what she wanted. The last present. *This had got to be it,* Lola thought to herself. She'd been hinting all year, she opened the box, out jumped a puppy. 'Finally,' she said, 'my own dog Rover!'

Rose Foster (11)
St Joseph's RC Primary School, Sunderland

The Magic Room

The room was empty, my puppy had gone, I thought she would have been here. I told her that I needed to go to the shops and then Lucy would be waiting for me. Ah! See there's a rattling box down there. It might be my puppy! I found her.

Josina James (11)
St Joseph's RC Primary School, Sunderland

The Scorching Desert

Peter walked through the desert, scorching heat was beating down on his bare chest. He struggled on, searching for his destination. He felt like he would never get back to normal life again. Suddenly the light left his eyes and he fell to his knees … panting for breath, but relieved.

Patrick Baldasera (11)
St Joseph's RC Primary School, Sunderland

The Final

There were only three minutes left. The corner was about to be taken, the crowd was silent. Ryan Giggs took the corner, the ball flew like a jet, Wayne Rooney headed it past Petr Cech like a rocket. The crowd roared. *Goal!*

Joe Ardley (11)
St Joseph's RC Primary School, Sunderland

Old House

Down my lane was the oldest house in history, or so it seemed to me. Something was spotted in that house, trying to find Mrs Brown's old treasure. Suddenly everything went quiet, I could hear a heart thump. Something strange was going on and I was going to find out.

Hannah Murphy (11)
St Joseph's RC Primary School, Sunderland

Golden Room

The wooden door slammed shut behind her. The whole room was gold. Bella took a deep breath and slowly walked forward. There she saw a path leading up to a small room. She stepped inside. There she saw a box. She opened it. *Wow!* A gold ring!

Anjana Varghese (11)
St Joseph's RC Primary School, Sunderland

207

Yummy

Humpty Dumpty went to the market so he could get a great, big target, before he knew it, he was squashed like a small Chewit. Soon you will be having scrambled egg and lovely tulips.

Abbie Green (11)
St Joseph's RC Primary School, Sunderland

The Three Birds And The Big Bad Crocodile

Once upon a time there lived three birds, they were old enough to build their own houses, one made of fruit, one leaves and one twigs. One day, a big bad crocodile blew down their houses, but the birds started to throw bits and pieces of their houses at him.

Sophie Reid (10)
Saltburn Primary School

The End

I could hear a distant roaring, I moved closer
raring for adventure. I proceeded cautiously
around a corner, I stopped, I stared, in front of
me was a huge red monster. It approached me,
I started to run, but I was too late. It had me.

Eve Wilkinson-Bell (10)
Saltburn Primary School

The First Squirrel In Space

Blast-off! His mission; to rid the Earth of poisonous popcorn; his name; Nuts. Oh yes, did I mention he's a squirrel who could hardly reach the controls? 'Release the popcorn,' said Nuts.
'We're out of fuel and heading into the sun!' said Bugs.
'The things we do for comedy!'

Connor Marshall (10)
Saltburn Primary School

211

A Pencil Pot Disaster

There I was sitting reading a book, I was too engaged to respond to anyone, but the moment was coming. I could feel an unpleasant coldness on the back of my neck, people were talking around me, my instinct telling, me I turned.
That was the pencil pot disaster.

Cerys Hambley (10)
Saltburn Primary School

The Open Sea

As Alex slept, the birds started singing. He stirred, a bang startled him, the boat had snapped in two, he fell into the sea. He grabbed a piece of wood and body-surfed to the nearest land. He looked up, two glowing eyes got closer.

'Wake up,' shouted his mum.

Matthew Donlan (10)
Saltburn Primary School

213

The Mood

There was a stamp, it went silent, and the door opened and the mood ran into the classroom. A book went flying across the room. What does the mood look like? Well he has long hair and a big head, his name is the funniest and stupid, it's Justin Time.

Oskar Frere-Smith (10)
Saltburn Primary School

Truth Or Mystery?

I was drowning, drowning in the deep blue sea,
screaming for my life, 'I'm too young to die.'
I saw a ship in the distance, it was coming
closer. 'Argh!' I was drowning in the Bermuda
Triangle.
'Get out now, Sophie, dry yourself off, it's
bedtime.'
'Thank goodness,' I whispered.

Sophie Legg (9)
Saltburn Primary School

The Spell

'Ert!' Wollick shouted, the hybrid dog-fox made a strange beast. It roared, Wollick ran down the corridor and tripped. It roared again as it ran towards him, claws like knives. He shouted, 'Ert.' The reverse spell rang out. The dog-fox separated. Wollick signed with relief as day ended.

Ben Corner (10)
Saltburn Primary School

Hunted

Mike felt his heart beat faster as the beast staggered closer. He thought the coast was clear, he ran to a nearby cave, was something leering? Mike discovered a dead man holding a radio in the cave. He quickly sent a message SOS, would the beast destroy him?

Jonathan Keeler (10)
Saltburn Primary School

Death And Birth

Albert knew there was not long until his death.
Memories of dancing with his wife, racing with
his children, working as a teacher flashed
through his head. Fading, they disappeared. He
closed his eyes, let death creep upon him.
The day that Albert died, his new grandchild,
Sunny, was born.

Gabrielle Taylor (9)
Saltburn Primary School

Aliens On Mars!

I met aliens once on Mars, they gave me this watch called a Bobble, they said, 'Use it in emergencies.' They knew a black hole was coming, they strapped themselves to the planet, but not me, I flew in, thought I was gonna die. Three, two, one …
'Simon wake up.'

Simon Hadden (10)
Saltburn Primary School

War

I woke up; *where am I? The Germans are attacking, get to the bomb shelter now.*
The siren goes off. The aeroplanes dropping bombs whenever they can.
Five hours later, broken houses. *What happened out here anyway?*
I enjoyed singing in the bomb shelter. That was really good.

Richard Pendry (10)
Saltburn Primary School

Doctor Who Puff

Kits was jealous of Professor Jaha, so she
savaged his work by mixing false liquid!
The Doctor walked in followed by Martha. 'This
is dodgy, false liquid,' remarked the doctor!
Suddenly sparks flew everywhere.
'System overload.' The Doctor flew into action,
jammed the system. 'Get out!' They ran to the
TARDIS.

Ellen Wilkinson (10)
Saltburn Primary School

221

The Woods

Me and my friends went for a water fight in the
woods, starting from 3 o'clock.
Soon it was dark, we were hearing funny,
howling noises, then … footsteps getting
louder. Oh no, it grabbed me. 'Ben, Ben, wake
up, are you awake?'

Ben Harrington (10)
Saltburn Primary School

Footie On My PS2

It was the World Cup, England vs Brazil. I
approached the ball, I nutmegged Kaka. The
crowd shouted 'Ole.' Some trickery to get
Ronaldhino. I shot it, heading for the top corner.
Would the keeper get a hand to it?
'Alex get off that PS2.'
But that was really cool!

Alex Sparrow (9)
Saltburn Primary School

223

Cool

10, 9, 8, 7, 6, 5, 4, 3, 2, 1. 'I'm off,' I said. 'We're halfway to Neptune. What was that?' I asked. An alien came in, it said, 'It's time for the ceremony.' Music came out, we danced the moonwalk but it lacked atmosphere. Out of this world!

Zannah Sprague (10)
Saltburn Primary School

Ahsatan

Ahsatan is travelling through the space
continuum when suddenly she falls, tumbling
helplessly into the immense black vortex. She
scrambles out, fiercely fighting the monstrous
creatures which lurk within. Ahsatan's mission
is almost complete, when suddenly from the
void she hears, 'Natasha, get up.'
'Oh five more minutes, Mum, please.'

Natasha Graham (9)
Saltburn Primary School

225

My Bizarre Experiment!

Today we did a bizarre experiment about hair,
we planned it, we tried it. Then we had to wait
for a week.
We waited and waited but finally the day came.
'Oh no,' yelled the teacher, 'we've left it too
long.'
It had all gone terribly wrong.

Cari-Anne Markey (10)
Saltburn Primary School

Untitled

When I was three years old I jumped off a picnic table, *crack* went my arm. I went inside. 'Grab the car keys, Dave.'
My mum and dad took me to the hospital with my brother. I found out that I had shattered my arm. Ow, it hurt.

Abigail Harrison (10)
Saltburn Primary School

227

Don't Let The Dog In

Rose got a new dog called Molly, she loved her but the dog was strange.
That night her dad told her not to let the dog in her room, but she did. She dreamt about taking Molly for a walk. Suddenly Molly bit her. She awoke, 'Molly, don't kill me.'

Evan Pottage (10)
Saltburn Primary School

Running For Your Life

'Where am I? Help!'
Rustling sounds from the trees start to get
louder, footsteps are stomping. I ran, ran,
climbed up the ladder, heart beating, *thump*,
thump. I hear a cracking. Something flies out,
starts attacking. 'Mum I'm dying.'
'No you're not, now get up, it's time for school,
c'mon.'

Jenny Cook (10)
Saltburn Primary School

My Worst Holiday

Mike and his mum got on the plane, he was very excited. Soon it took off and was in the air for a few hours when it landed, Mike was asleep. He woke up, no one was on the plane, he walked off, everyone had gone. Mike cried.

Connor Watson (10)
Saltburn Primary School

The Unsolved Mystery Of Bones

Jake went down to the beach. He saw something in the sand. 'What's that?' He got his shovel and dug up bones, they started growing and turned into a skeleton. A skeleton with a sword, threatening Jake with it. Jake shouted, 'Help!'
The first act had ended.

Christopher Miloszewski (10)
Saltburn Primary School

The Dark Evening

One evening in the dark windy field there was an old grey house. Margaret and John lived with two children called Emily and Henry. When evening was turning into night, Emily said to Henry, 'Do you think Mum's going to sell the house?' They would find out the next day.

Chelsee Bottomley (10)
Saltburn Primary School

Devil's Land

Danny walked across the Devii's land, almost falling into one of the bottomless pits of darkness. Suddenly a lava monster tried to kill him. Luckily Danny had a sword with him, he sliced the monster's head off and lava squirted everywhere.

'James, get off your PlayStation …'

Katherine Judson (10)
Saltburn Primary School

The Three Blind Mice Get Food Poisoning

One day on a hill in a house lived three blind mice. That day evil Humpty Dumpty gave the mice a packet of Walkers cheddar cheese crisps. The three blind mice got food poisoning from the crisps. Humpty Dumpty went to jail and the mice got their tails chopped off.

Charlotte Walker (10)
Saltburn Primary School

Puss In Fruts

Once upon a time a notice went out for
catching rabbits for the king, so Puss did
it. When he was looking around he found a
wardrobe door. He opened it and looked inside.
It was a magic world. He spotted a rabbit stool
and ran for his life.

Louis Hiddleston (9)
Saltburn Primary School

Totuga, The Last Spanish Pirate Ship

Egonard was sat in his cabin aboard his galleon, The Eclipse. It had quad cannons and 250 crew. Egonard heard the man in the crow's nest roaring, 'Ship ahoy, ship ahoy.' Egonard ran out of his cabin and bellowed, 'Turn starboard and fire.' It turned and destroyed the barricade.

Joe Robson (10)
Saltburn Primary School

Twinkle Twinkle Little Egg

There was an egg called Humpty Dumpty who flew up to the sky. He met the moon and had a tea party. The moon was called Fred. He sent a message to Katie, the moon's arch enemy. She got the note, it said 'Peace between us and Earth.'
'OK Sun.'

Tyla Jones (9)
Saltburn Primary School

YoungWriters

Information

We hope you have enjoyed reading this book - and that
you will continue to enjoy it in the coming years.

If you like reading and writing, drop us a line or give
us a call and we'll send you a free information pack.
Alternatively visit our website at www.youngwriters.co.uk

Write to:
Young Writers Information,
Remus House,
Coltsfoot Drive,
Peterborough,
PE2 9JX
Tel: (01733) 890066
Email: youngwriters@forwardpress.co.uk